INDIANS OF ARIZONA

A Guide to Arizona's Heritage

Jeanne Broome   O'ODHAM BASKETMAKER JUANITA AHILL

A RENAISSANCE HOUSE PUBLICATION

By Eleanor H. Ayer

1999 Printing

ISBN: 1-55838-112-0

Renaissance House Publishers
A Division of Primer Publishers
5738 North Central Avenue
Phoenix, Arizona 85012

1-800-521-9221

Cover photo of Susie Yazzie and granddaughter weaving Navajo Yei Rug.
© Jerry Jacka

10 9 8 7 6 5 4

WELCOME

Arizona's Indian country—it has been called haunting, stunningly beautiful, fascinating, enriching. And like any cross-section of America, certain areas are primitive, desolate, and a bit depressing. But the overall effect on the traveler to Indian country is a sense of respect for the roots from which many Americans take their heritage. In this fast-paced age it is reassuring to be among people who can find a meaningful existence without total dependence on a high-tech world.

Arizona is home to a wider variety of Indian cultures than any other state in America. Here it is possible to watch native artisans at their crafts, enjoy ethnic foods, observe certain rituals and ceremonial dances. However, these privileges carry with them an accountability to respect the privacy and customs of residents. No alcohol, fireworks, firearms, and only limited photography on reservation lands. Ask before trespassing. Be respectful of property. Travel in good taste, as you would in any other area of the country.

This book is an overview of Arizona's Indian country. There is much more to be said about the history, culture, crafts, and contemporary lifestyles of Arizona's native people. The directory of organizations, museums, and trading posts in the back of this book is merely a sampling. For further reading, we suggest *Parks & Monuments of Arizona*, *Southwest Indian Arts & Crafts* and *A Guide to the Anasazi and Other Ancient Southwest Indians* (all in the American Traveler Series from Renaissance House.)

Our thanks in preparing **Indians of Arizona** goes to the tribal councils at each of the reservations highlighted in this book. Additionally, we must thank Tandy Young of the Native American Tourism Center and Tony Machukay of the Arizona Commission of Indian Affairs for reading the text prior to publication and making valuable suggestions in the interests of clarity and accuracy.

We ask you to keep in mind while reading that there is sometimes more than one spelling for many of the proper names. You may find Mohave or Mojave, Pascua or Pasqua. Tribal representatives for nearly all of the reservations in the book have approved each of the write ups. This is your assurance of the accuracy and quality of this guide to Arizona's Indian people.

CONTENTS

Prehistoric Indians

Protected within Arizona's national parks and monuments are some of the most fascinating Indian ruins in North America. The state's arid climate has helped to preserve many artifacts from prehistoric cultures.

Indians have inhabited this region for at least 10,000 years. The Cochise culture once dominated what is now southeastern Arizona. These were a very simple people who likely emigrated from Asia and probably gathered nuts and berries for food. There is evidence that they lived in the area until 500 B.C.

Evolving from the Cochise culture about the time of Christ were a people known for their advanced agricultural techniques. They lived in what is now southern Arizona. The later Pima Indians would call these people the Hohokam, meaning "those who have gone." The earliest period of Hohokam history lasted about 500 years. Evidence of the culture has been found on the Gila River Reservation near Chandler. These people were skilled stone workers.

From 600-900 A.D. was the Colonial Hohokam period. During this time these "primitive" people developed an amazing system of irrigation canals to water their arid homeland, the largest of which was 30 feet wide and 10 feet deep. The canals extended nearly 150 miles. The Hohokam also built ball courts and developed a distinctive pottery using a red dye on brown clay.

The period of 900-1200 was that of the Sedentary Hohokam. During this period some of the people moved north, into the present-day Flagstaff area. Their craftsmen did beautiful work with shells and their potters could now produce jars capable of holding 30 gallons of water. It was in this period that the Hohokam expanded their irrigation system. Along the Gila and Salt Rivers, their canals stretched more than 600 miles!

Today in the city of Phoenix you can see remains of these early Hohokam canals. City founders used the abandoned canals to bring the first water into their new community. Like the ancient bird for whom it was named, the city was reborn from the "ashes" of these early people.

The peak years of the Hohokam culture were approximately 1200-1400, what historians call "The Golden Age of Southern Arizona." The greatest achievement of those years was in architecture. Houses were expanded to two stories, some accessible only by

Jeanne Broome   MONUMENT VALLEY PETROGLYPH

ladders. Ruins of these homes can be seen today at Casa Grande National Monument south of Phoenix.

About this time another prehistoric culture, the Salado, moved south into Hohokam territory. For nearly 300 years they had farmed the Salt River Valley to the north (Salado means "salty" in Spanish). The Salado were not war-like and may, in fact, have been the inspiration for the elaborate new Hohokam architecture, for the Salado had developed 40-room two-story structures. They were known also for their finely woven and elaborately dyed textiles.

Shortly after 1400, the Hohokam lived up to their name. Historians are not certain what caused their disappearance, but they believe that today's Pima and Papago (Tohono O'odham) Indians are their descendants. The Salado disappeared about the same time. Their culture is preserved today at Tonto National Monument east of Phoenix. Here you can see beads, shells, pieces of pottery, cradleboards, clothing, and many other Salado artifacts.

Classic among prehistoric cultures were the Anasazi or "ancient ones." Historians usually divide the Anasazi into two periods. The earlier culture, The Basketmakers, inhabited several regions of the Southwest until 700 A.D. As their name suggests, the culture of these people revolved around their baskets. Usually made of willow woven in coils, the baskets were of such perfect construction that they could carry 2-3 gallons of water. Others were used for cooking. The standard "all-

5

purpose" baskets looked more like trays and measured anywhere from 3 inches to 3 feet across.

The Basketmakers raised corn and squash as well as gathering fruits, bulbs and the like for their meals. They hunted small game and even constructed snares for this purpose. One snare found near Kayenta weighed 28 pounds and was rigged with nearly four *miles* of string! For capturing larger game, the Basketmakers fashioned a spear-like device called an *atlatl.* Clothing was simple and sparse: sandals made of yucca fibers, loin cloths for the men, and juniper bark diapers for baby.

About 400 A.D., these Basketmakers began building houses rather than living in shallow caves as they had previously. The earliest models were called pit houses, the pits being 3 to 5 feet deep and surrounded by poles covered with dried mud. Entry was via an underground passage. This culture was still very basket-oriented, but pottery was introduced about this time as well.

Pictographs and other evidences of the Basketmakers' culture may be seen at Canyon de Chelly, a national monument in northeastern Arizona. At one of the park sites, Canyon del Muerto (Canyon of the Dead), visitors can learn much about the death rituals of these people. Among other customs, these Anasazi buried with their dead a pair or two of new, finely fashioned sandals.

By the early part of the 9th century, the Anasazi culture had evolved into what the later Spaniards called "Pueblo," meaning community. The primitive houses-- now with more than one room--were built of a sort of masonry. "Kivas" replaced the underground portions of the houses. These kivas had specialized functions. Often they were used for ceremonial or religious gatherings at which only males were allowed.

Although these people still made baskets, they began to use more and more pottery. Their pottery was of a higher quality than earlier generations, and the typical design that began to emerge was the black and white pattern. Cotton was introduced as the new cultivation crop. From it, blankets and clothing articles were woven.

The heyday of the Anasazi culture was during the Great Pueblo period. This began shortly after the year 1000 and lasted nearly 300 years. It was during this time that the great prehistoric "apartment" houses were constructed. Some were five stories high and had dozens of rooms. Remains of these structures can be seen today at Navajo National Monument, located on the Navajo reservation. Stone tools, pottery and cliff dwellings in the Grand Canyon indicate the presence of the Anasazi there about 1000 years ago.

Jeanne Broome   KIVAS IN CANYON DE CHELLY

For reasons still uncertain--but pointing most likely to drought--the Anasazi had, by 1300 A.D., abandoned their southwest homes. From Keet Seel and Betatakin (in present-day Navajo National Monument) to what is now the bottomland of the canyons surrounding Lake Powell, the Anasazi vanished. Some historians believe they were driven off by wandering tribes who sought the stores of food in the Anasazi granaries.

Quite a different culture from the Anasazi or Hohokam was the Mogollon (MUGGY-own). These people also had their roots in the early Cochise culture. By 300-200 B.C. they were well-established in east-central Arizona. The first Mogollon people built pit houses and gathered berries and roots for food. Even the earliest Mogollon had extremely well-made pottery, leaving historians to surmise that knowledge of this craft may have come from Mexico.

Gradually these people became hunters, using bows and arrows, and there is evidence of some farming. Near the end of the Mogollon era--during the Mimbres period--the society changed greatly. Dwellings were now apartment houses from one to three stories high, with 40 or 50 rooms, gathered in pueblos. The Anasazi, who moved into the area toward the end of the period, may have influenced this architectural innovation. But by the start of the 14th century, the Mogollon, like their Anasazi neighbors, had vanished from the area.

About the time that the Anasazi culture reigned in what is now northeastern Arizona, the Sinagua people inhabited today's Verde Valley. Their name in Spanish means "without water," as indeed they often were. These people farmed the dry, rocky land around present-day Flagstaff for hundreds of years before the eruption of a great volcano about 1066. The volcano deposited a black ash on the countryside that proved very fertile and ultimately brought some Anasazi and Hohokam to live here as well. Today Sunset Crater is a national monument.

Early Sinaguans lived in pit houses, the pits being quite deep. But the later people built large and elaborate dwellings among the cliffs. One of the most spectacular is preserved today at Montezuma Castle. It is five stories high with 20 rooms, built about 1100. The foot-thick ceiling beams have helped keep the structure in nearly as good condition as the day it was built.

Near this national monument is Montezuma Well, a limestone sink which was used for irrigation by the Sinaguans and by the Hohokam nearly 500 years before them. To the northwest is Tuzigoot National Monument, Tuzigoot being the Apache word for "crooked water." Here, about 1125 A.D., lived a community of Sinaguans who occupied more than 70 rooms beneath the cliffs. The Sinaguans lived in these pueblos until the early 1400's when, like their contemporaries, drought or an equal force caused them to leave the area.

The period from 1400 to 1625 produced some of the most spectacular pottery ever made in the Southwest. Hopi Indians (who today live in northeastern Arizona) created a black design over yellow. They also made a polychrome pottery using beautiful geometric patterns as well as shapes of living things. Backgrounds were often yellow with designs in red or black.

Forty years into the 16th century, Arizona's Indians experienced a major change in their culture: the arrival of the Spanish. Life for the red man would never be the same. There had been rumblings in Mexico for several years about the wealth to be found in the north. Streets in the mythical Seven Cities of Cibola were said to be paved with gold--there simply for the taking.

So it was that in 1540 explorer Francisco Coronado arrived in present-day Arizona near Bisbee. The party found no gold, but it did find natives to convert to Christianity. Franciscan friars worked first among the Papago Indians. The missions they built were the first permanent structures of the white man in this area.

The mission period of Arizona's history is preserved today at Tumacacori National Monument. The Tumacacori mission and nearby San Xavier del Bac were part of a chain of missions established by the Jesuit missionary Father Eusebio Francisco Kino. They

Arizona Office of Tourism   MONTEZUMA CASTLE

are still in use today. Father Kino was beloved by the Indians and is said to have traveled 75,000 miles in Arizona during his 24 years there.

In 1692 a mission was established near today's city of Nogales. That same year the Indian lands were claimed by Spain. Without the sophisticated weaponry of their Spanish rivals, the natives could not defend their lands. Neither could they defend themselves against the strange new diseases that the white man brought with him. The decline of Indian dominance in the Southwest had begun.

By 1821, the Indian lands were under the rule of Mexico. During the next 20 years, white American trappers and traders headed west in search of beaver to satisfy the new fashion crazes of wealthy easterners. Though they mapped and surveyed Indian lands, they were not immediately threatening to the natives. But at the end of the Mexican War in 1848, the Indian lands came under U.S. domination.

It didn't take long for Americans to head west to explore this new territory. During the gold rush to California in 1849, many prospectors passed through Indian country. With the establishment of the Butterfield Overland mail route through Tucson and the arrival of the white man in larger numbers, the natives felt their lands increasingly threatened. By the late 1850's, the Indian/white conflict was reaching major proportions.

The fires of warfare were finally ignited in 1861 when rancher John Ward accused Chief Cochise and the Chiricahua Apaches of kidnapping his wife's half-breed son. In truth, Ward himself had beaten the boy so severely that he left home. But Lt. George Bascom chose to believe Ward and marched--with 54 soldiers--to Apache Pass, homeland of Cochise. Confronted by Bascom and his men, Cochise escaped, but several of his people did not. By nightfall, the Apaches were poised to attack a wagon train traveling over the pass. Bascom retaliated by having some of Cochise's band hanged, whereupon the Apache chief declared war on all Americans living in what is now Arizona.

The Apaches were considered the fiercest of the southwest tribes, but American intrusion ultimately brought the Navajo and other peaceful Arizona Indians to rebellion. One by one, they gave in to their inevitable fates at the hands of the American government. But there were four tribes who were determined not to go without a fight.

Kit Carson, under orders from the U.S. government, lay siege to the Navajo homelands. Fighting and deprivation continued endlessly. At last the American victors rounded up the remnants of this once mighty nation and ordered them on their infamous "Long Walk" to New Mexico's *Bosque Redondo*. There they were reduced by disease, starvation and inhumane treatment to a fraction of their original number. At last realizing what they had perpetrated, the government allowed those who lived to return to their Arizona homelands under the terms of a treaty in 1868.

One year later the Hualapais gave up. In 1875 the Yavapais surrendered and by 1881 the Western Apaches had been subdued. In truth, it was largely the government's enlistment of turncoat Apaches to its own ranks that finally brought the Arizona tribes to defeat.

As for Cochise, Indian agent Tom Jeffords--a friend of the Indians and highly successful ambassador--was able finally to enact a peace. Under the terms of the agreement, the traditional Chiricahua Apache lands were set aside as their reservation. Cochise was free to live within this territory, where he died in 1874.

Arizona's Native Americans were ultimately distributed on 20 reservations throughout the state. The 14 tribes that today populate Arizona account for 14 percent of all Indians in America. Although more than 19 million acres of land is designated for Indian reservations, only half of the state's 160,000 Indians now live on them. The two largest Indian reservations in the U.S. today are within Arizona: the Navajo and the Tohono O'odham (formerly Papago).

Jeanne Broome   NAVAJO CRAFTS

THE NAVAJO

Largest of all Indian reservations in America is the Navajo, which occupies much of the northeastern Arizona plateau and stretches into Utah and New Mexico as well. Nearly 140,000 Navajo live on the reservation today. Many of Arizona's most spectacular geologic and archaeological wonders are here: Rainbow Bridge at Lake Powell, Canyon de Chelly, Monument Valley and more. The Navajo Nation has five population centers in Arizona: Chinle, the Window Rock/Fort Defiance area, Leupp, Tuba City, and Kayenta.

Entering Navajo country from the north, you will see signs to the reservation's largest city, Shiprock, which is just across the Arizona border in New Mexico. Long before you see the signs you'll spot the giant rock for which the town is named, a monolith visible from Colorado. Your route south through Arizona will take you first to Chinle, gateway to Canyon de Chelly National Monument. Chinle is a major population center on the reservation, with chain stores, elementary and secondary schools, and many public services.

About 30 miles south is Ganado, site of the Hubbell Trading Post National Historic Site. The post is in operation today as it has been for nearly 100 years. Visitors may purchase Navajo jewelry, wool rugs, and other hand-crafted items.

The capital of the Navajo Nation is at Window Rock, in the southeast corner of the reservation. In the Tribal Council building is a room designed to look like a hogan*. Here the governing body or Tribal Council meets. Nearly half of Window Rock's residents are employed in some type of public administration. The Bureau of Indian Affairs has a big office here as well.

Standing as a backdrop to Tribal Headquarters is *Tseghahodzanil*, "the rock with the hole in it." Measuring 47 feet in diameter, this unique formation is the result of hundreds of years of wind and other erosion. Also of interest in town is the fairgrounds, site each September of the Navajo Tribal Fair. At the fair (one of the largest in the U.S.) visitors can watch native dancing, eat traditional Navajo foods such as fry bread, and purchase Navajo arts and crafts. The Tribal Zoo, also in Window Rock, features animals native to the reservation. Adjacent to it is an excellent museum devoted to Navajo history and displaying native crafts and artifacts.

Just six miles north of Window Rock is Fort Defiance. It was from here, in 1863, that Colonel Kit Carson directed his Navajo Campaign, which ultimately ended in the "Long Walk" to New Mexico. Today the Window Rock/Ft. Defiance area shares much of the activity of the Navajo Nation with nearby Gallup, New Mexico, 24 miles away.

In the southwestern corner of the reservation is Leupp, a city of rapid growth, situated on the Little Colorado River. For the traveler, there is much to see in the area: Meteor Crater, the Painted Desert, Sunset Crater, Walnut Canyon, Canyon Diablo and the spectacular San Francisco Peaks. The closest major city is Winslow, 29 miles to the south.

Continuing in a clockwise loop around the reservation's population centers, you come next to Tuba City. Its Indian name, *Tonanesdizi*, means "tangled waters," for underground are many springs which make the area an oasis. Just east of Tuba City is the Hopi Reservation, surrounded completely by the Navajo Reservation. Each year in late October, Tuba City hosts the Western Navajo Fair.

The next major city is Kayenta, famous as the gateway to spectacular Monument Valley. This beautiful country is filled with awesome red rock formations which stretch for miles through northeastern Arizona. Kayenta is only a short distance from Navajo National Monument, site of some of the finest Anasazi ruins.

---

* HOGAN: a hexagonal or octagonal Navajo dwelling built of logs and sticks covered with mud, sod or adobe and with the door facing east.

Jeanne Broome   NAVAJO HOGAN

The spiritual Black Mesa area is just south of Kayenta.
Along the highway you can see evidence of Black Mesa
Pipeline and Peabody Coal, two major employers in the
area. Much of the tribe's income is derived from large
oil and natural gas reserves.

The Navajo are a determined, persistent people
with a desire to improve their lifestyle. In Navajo
society, women are much respected and there are close
ties between families by marriage. Religion remains an
important force in Navajo life.

Navajo craftsmen are best known for their fine
silver/turquoise jewelry and for their textiles. While
there is some evidence that prehistoric southwest
Indians used turquoise, it was not until the mid-19th
century and the opening of the Santa Fe Trail that the
Navajo became skilled jewelers. They borrowed some
of their designs from other cultures. Concha belts were
likely an influence of the Plains Indians. The well-
known squash blossom came from Mexico. But
authentically Navajo is the *Ketoh* or bowguard,
originally worn on the wrist when shooting a bow, now
a popular piece of jewelry.

At first, Navajo jewelry was made only of silver.
Turquoise found its way into use about 1890. Much of
the turquoise in America comes from mines in the
southwest. Early designs often utilized only one stone,
and this is still a trademark of the Navajo.

Many stories surround turquoise. It is a harbinger
of good health and fortune. To insure a pleasant day,
look at a turquoise when you first rise. And if you

13

mistrust your spouse's fidelity, give him or her a piece of turquoise, then watch carefully for signs of the stone's fading. That loss of color is said to be confirmation of your worst fears!

Weaving has been a part of Navajo life since the late 1700's, but few examples exist from those early years. From 1800-1850, while travel and trading were heavy along the Santa Fe Trail, weaving flourished. Blankets were major trade items. The most frequently used colors were red, black, white and blue. Stripes, zig-zags, and diamond shapes were traditional Navajo patterns. One of the most highly prized items was the chief's blanket, so-called because of its importance but not limited to use by the chief. This blanket was always wider than it was long and featured large horizontal black and white bands. Later designs incorporated terraced diamonds and triangles, and the patterns were ultimately used in rug making.

When the railroad penetrated Arizona in the 1800's, bringing as part of its cargo machine-made textiles and clothing from the east, the demand for Navajo handcrafted items diminished. But the eastern influence was not entirely negative. Navajo weavers began experimenting with brighter colors in their wool. They borrowed designs from some of the imported Oriental rugs, which are still evident in the work from craftsmen of the Ganado and Four Corners areas. In fact, Teec Nos Pos is today the major center of Navajo rug making. One of the styles is called "sandpainting rug" because sandpaintings are such an important part of the Navajo ceremonials.

Sandpaintings are not distinctly Navajo, but the Navajo people use them the most as part of their curing rite. As the name implies, the pictures are made of very finely ground minerals, charcoal, and even pollen or corn meal. There are hundreds of designs, many of them depicting spirits. The sick or injured sits on the sandpainting and lets the sand absorb the evils that are causing his illness. That accomplished, the sand is buried. Paintings used for healing are made and destroyed within one day. The colors in a sandpainting indicate direction: blue=south; black=north; yellow=west; white=east; red symbolizes sunshine.

Today as you drive through the Navajo reservation, you will find large areas of extreme isolation between the population centers. Hogans and government houses occasionally appear. From time to time you encounter temporary roadside stands selling hand-crafted items. And in nearly every town is a trading post which offers local goods, often at lower prices than in the larger areas.

Jeanne Broome   KACHINA DOLLS

THE HOPI

Surrounded completely by the Navajo reservation, the gentle, perservering Hopis live quietly on 910,000 acres in northeastern Arizona. Home to nearly 10,000 Hopi Indians, the reservation boundaries have for decades been marked by border disputes with the Navajo which are still unresolved.

Legend says that the Hopi, over several generations, emerged from the underworld to begin occupying the Black Mesa area where they have lived since. Today the Hopi reservation encompasses three mesas, proceeding from east to west: First Mesa, Second Mesa, and Third Mesa. In the early days when defense was a major consideration, the Hopi built their villages on the mesa tops. Old Oraibi, on the top of Third Mesa, is thought to be the oldest community of constant habitation in the U.S., established about 1150. The natives believe these mesas to be the center of the universe.

Many consider the Hopi to be the thinkers and scholars among Native American peoples. Religion and tradition are extremely important to them and they are greatly opposed to change which might jeopardize these values. Central to their religion are the Hopi Kachinas, of which the dolls are only one aspect. Kachinas are supernatural spirits which live in the minds of the people. The kachina dolls are used for

15

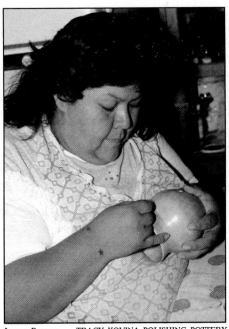

Jeanne Broome   TRACY KOVINA POLISHING POTTERY

instructing children in the Hopi ways. There are more than 200 kachinas, of which about 30 are central to the religion.

Ceremonials are held from the winter solstice to October. The public is welcome for it is felt that these events are for the good of all people. Exhibits at the tribally owned Hopi Cultural Center express the many aspects of Hopi culture. Crafts, clothing, and displays showing the uniqueness among different Hopi villages are the focus of the Center.

When you visit, remember that the Hopi allow <u>no</u> recording or photographing of religious events. Alcohol is universally forbidden. Take time to stop at the many craft centers, for the Hopi are excellent potters and silversmiths. Their overlay style, developed in the 1930's, has become distinctively Hopi. These craftsmen also produce beautiful multi-colored pottery, characterized by the Hopi yellow/orange clay base. Although basketry is now the least practiced of the Native Indian crafts, the Hopis still produce many baskets for gifts and personal use.

Because of their location within the Navajo reservation, the Hopi are isolated from business centers. The major employers are the government bureaus which administer Indian affairs on the reservation. Crafts and retail businesses employ about 20% of the reservation's people.

PIPE SPRING NATIONAL MONUMENT

THE KAIBAB - PAIUTE

Just under 300 Paiute people live on the 120,413-acre Kaibab-Paiute reservation of northwestern Arizona. They have been called "Diggers," for in earlier times the people dug roots and gathered berries and nuts for food, rather than pursuing farming. There are five villages on the reservation today. Because of its remoteness, the people are able to successfully preserve their cultural and linguistic ties to the past.

In the solitude of this beautiful area, the Paiutes still produce baskets. They are best known for their shallow Wedding Baskets. But the native materials are increasingly hard to find and basketry no longer contributes much to the Indians' economy. Most employed Paiutes work in government services.

One of the reservation's main attractions is Pipe Spring National Monument, once the only dependable source of water for 60 miles. Mormon missionaries camped here in 1858. In the early 1870's, Brigham Young built a fort on the site. Arizona's first telegraph station operated in Pipe Spring until 1923, when the area became a national monument. A museum featuring Paiute history and culture is being developed.

The reservation operates an RV park and the Kaibab-Paiute Educational hiking trail. Reservation Steamboat Rock is one of the geologic highlights of the area.

Jeanne Broome   HAVASUPAI LOADING SUPPLIES

THE HAVASUPAI

Three thousand feet below the rim of the Grand Canyon live the 500 Indians of the Havasupai tribe. Their people have lived at the canyon bottom—actually in a side canyon of the Grand called Havasu—for the last 700 years. The reservation's single village of Supai is the last location in the U.S. where mail is still delivered by mule. Mule, horse, or foot power are the only means of ground transportation to this remote community, some eight miles down a steep trail.

For all its remoteness, some 20,000 people a year visit the Havasupai land. This pristine countryside can accommodate only a limited number of visitors at a time, so reservations must be made well in advance. Tourism is the principal means of income on the reservation. In contrast to the wealthy retirement communities elsewhere in Arizona, the average income of a Havasupai family is $2500 a year.

Wealth, for these people, lies in the beauty of their lands, for this reservation is known as the Shangri-la of the Grand Canyon. Running into the canyon here is Havasu Creek which, before joining the Colorado River, cascades down several beautiful waterfalls. The most spectacular are the Havasu, the Mooney and the Navajo. The travertine hollows at the bases of these falls fill with a gorgeous blue-green water to offer absolutely breathtaking scenery. Ancestors of the Coconino Indians, the Havasupai reservation is located in Arizona's modern day Coconino County.

18

Mast Enterprises   EARLENE HAVATONE, MS. HUALAPAI

THE HUALAPAI

"**P**eople of the Tall Pine," as the Hualapai are known, occupy nearly a million acres in northwestern Arizona along the south rim of the Grand Canyon. Many of the 1100+ inhabitants live in the reservation's only town, (and tribal headquarters), Peach Springs, the only road access to the Grand Canyon for many miles.

The Hualapai are much like their eastern neighbors, the Havasupai. For centuries both were hunters and gatherers. The Hualapai once lived in the northeastern part of today's Arizona. Early settlers found them afraid, hard-working people. But government demands and treaty violations increased. The peace was ultimately shattered when the government moved the Hualapai from their cool homelands to the desert-like Colorado River Basin.

Today, back on the high plateaus of the Grand Canyon, the tribe oversees a livestock herd and ranching is second only to the government as an employer. The Hualapai River Runners operate popular rafting and float trips through the Grand Canyon. An intriguing natural feature is the Grand Canyon Caverns--huge subterranean "rooms" located 21 stories underground. Fishing and hunting are also abundant in the area. The fortunate visitor to the Hualapai reservation can witness the occasional bird dances in which the dancers seem to be floating as they move back and forth in beautiful flowing, beaded dresses.

Fort Mojave Indian Tribe

Needles, the California city that often tops U.S. heat records, is also tribal headquarters for the Mojave Indians. The Fort Mojave reservation straddles the California-Arizona-Nevada border along the Colorado River. The majority of the reservation lies in Arizona where just over 600 people live "The People By The River", they call themselves.

Here the sun shines *99 percent* of the time! With a 255-day growing season, agriculture is important to the Mojave, although irrigation is a must in this desert climate.

Earliest historical records show the Mojave living along this same section of the Colorado River. They were peaceful people until the Spanish arrived and attempted to change their way of life. But with the Spanish influx, they became increasingly war-like and highly feared.

The Mojave had few religious rituals pertaining to crops. In religious matters, they placed great significance on dreams which they believed were the source of special powers. The Colorado River Indian reservation (further south) is home to a segment of Mojave people as well.

Three-fourths of all reservation jobs are related to the operation of the tribe. The Mojave people are known for their pottery and beadwork which can be purchased on the reservation. Hunting and fishing opportunities on the reservation draw many visitors.

Ronald Moore   BLUE WATER MARINA BEACH

COLORADO RIVER RESERVATION

More than eighty percent of the Colorado River Indian Reservation is located in Arizona, with the remainder in California. People of the Mojave, Chemehuevi, Hopi and Navajo tribes make up its membership, with tribal headquarters approximately one mile southwest of Parker.

Dams along the Colorado have stabilized the river's flow, making this portion a recreational paradise. The attendant lodges, marinas, restaurants, concessions, and mobile home parks contribute to the reservation's economy. Agriculture also is a major contributor. But the majority of the tribal labor force is employed by the various governments associated with the reservation.

This is the oldest Indian reservation in Arizona, created in 1865 by executive order of President Chester A. Arthur. It contains two National Historic Sites; the oldest Mohave Presbyterian Mission and the once prosperous gold mining town of La Paz, now mostly a memory. The tribe operates a fascinating museum which is responsible for preserving and displaying the artifacts and culture of the reservation's tribes.

Public events include the National Indian Days Celebration in September and an All Indian Rodeo held in December each year. Each of the Colorado River tribes has its own arts and crafts, including baskets, pottery, bead work, silver jewelry, kachina dolls and woven rugs.

The Sovereign Nation of the Cocopahs

Xawitt Kunyavaei

THE COCOPAH

This reservation is divided into east, west and north reservations which house nearly 660 tribal members. Traditionally the Cocopah are part of the Yuman Tribes. At one time they were joined with the Maricopa and Yuma as one. But by the late 1700's the Cocopah had broken with their associates. Although they live in arid desert country, they have farmed the fertile Colorado River area for many years.

While economic development is limited, cultural attractions abound. Spring brings Cocopah Festivity Days, featuring traditional dancing and food such as fry bread and Indian tacos. Cocopah artisans display gourd rattles, beadwork and other crafts, and Miss Cocopah is crowned.

Dancers entertain in the Dance Grounds on the east reservation where there is a large area for singing. The excellent Cocopah singers perform all over the southwest and have particularly beautiful memorial programs which they present at private funeral services. On two segments of the reservation are "Cry Houses" which are utilized only for funerals.

The Cocopah Elders have an active program. They operate a reconstructed 1800's Indian Village at the end of a tourist train running from Yuma to the reservation. Here they sell many native crafts including the unique ribbonshirts and ribbon dresses.

FORT YUMA

Yuma Crossing on the Colorado River in far southwestern Arizona is the site of many major historical events in the Old West. This gateway to the California missions and gold fields was opened to white settlers by the area's native people, the Quechan (KWE-shan) Indians. The oft-repeated story of bitter conflict between the native Indians and the Anglo intruders who expected them to submit to the white man's cultural and governmental demands resulted in the Quechan being sent to a reservation. Their vigorous protests against being moved to the Mojave reservation did result in the establishment of the Fort Yuma reservation, now home to 2350 tribal members.

The Quechan are attempting to preserve their heritage through the Quechan Heritage Site, located across the river from the Yuma Crossing National Historic Landmark, a part of which is also on the reservation. The museums will interpret many of the same historical events, but from two decidedly different perspectives.

The 44,000-acre reservation straddles the state boundary with California. In nearby Yuma are the Territorial Prison and the Fort Yuma Quartermaster Depot state parks. Each year in March, the Quechan Tribe hosts a major pow-wow which draws native dancers from across the U.S.

MARYLAND CartoGraphics, INC.
Columbia, Maryland 21045

NEVADA

UT

Littlefield

3 Kaibab
Indian
Reservation

Freed

Jacob

Kaibab
Fo

Lake Mead

Lake Mead
National Recreation
Area

Lake Mead
National
Recreation
Area

Havasupai
Indian
Reservation

4

5

Hualapai Indian
Reservation

93

66

Seligman

40

Ash Fork

68

Kingman

Yavapai-
Prescott
Indian
Reservation

89

Ka

93

Prescott

10

CALIFORNIA

Fort Mohave
Indian
Reservation

6

National

Bagdad

Prescott

Lake Havasu
City

95

Kirkland

Hillside

Fores

| 0 | 10 | 20 | 30 | 40 | 50 | Miles |
| 0 | 10 | 20 | 30 | 40 | 50 | Kilometers |

Parker

Bill Williams River

Congress

Colorado
River
Indian
Reservation

7

72

Aguila

Wickenburg

71

60

Vicksburg

60

89

74

Ehrenberg

10

Gle

Yuma

95

Kofa
National
Wildlife
Refuge

Tonopah

Sonora

Buckeye

Proving

85

Grounds

Desert

Ak-
Ind
Res

Fort
Yuma
Indian
Reservation

9

Gila Bend

Yuma

Gila

Dateland

8

Cocopah
Indian
Reservation

Welton

Tacna

Luke Air Force Range

85

San Luis

Cabeza Prieta
National Wildlife
Refuge

Ajo

Why

Toh

86

Organ Pipe
Cactus
National
Monument

85

Lukeville

ARIZONA'S INDIAN RESERVATIONS:

Ak-Chin	18
Camp Verde	11
Cocopah	8
Colorado River	7
Fort Apache	12
Fort McDowell	15
Fort Mohave	6
Fort Yuma	9
Gila River	17
Havasupai	4
Hopi	2
Hualapai	5
Kaibab-Paiute	3
Navajo	1

Pasqua Yaqui	20
Salt River	16
San Carlos	14
San Xavier	21
Tohono O'odham	19
Tonto Apache	13
Yavapai-Prescott	10

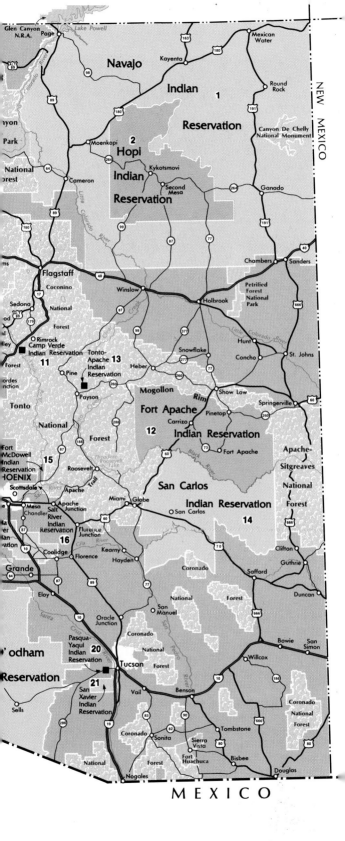

IRIS JONES, POW-WOW PRINCESS

YAVAPAI-PRESCOTT RESERVATION

Fewer than 116 tribal members now inhabit this tiny reservation located on the north side of the city of Prescott. But for hundreds of years the Yavapai lived as hunters and gatherers in a vast 10-million-acre area of central and western Arizona. Although there were three divisions of Yavapai, now known as the Fort McDowell and Camp Verde Yavapai, they considered themselves to be one people who spoke the same language and shared the same culture.

The men were great hunters and were sought after by the Hopi to trade for buckskins, rams' horns and pigments used in their ceremonies. The women collected mescal and plants such as yucca which made a fine natural detergent. Throughout the years the women have crafted beautiful baskets which are displayed in many museums.

Today the Yavapai-Prescott Tribe has developed a segment of its reservation in an effort to realize economic security and jobs for its members. The developed portion houses a 162-room hotel, bingo enterprise, smoke shop, service station and convenience market. Plans are being completed to develop a cultural heritage center to preserve the history of the tribe for its youth. The tribe also hosts an annual Inter-Tribal pow-wow open to the public.

CAMP VERDE

Approximately 700 Yavapai and Tonto Apache now live on the Camp Verde reservation. The Yavapai-Apache are descendants of the fierce groups who invaded from the north between 1000-1800 A.D. Until 1871, hostile Yavapai-Apaches raided what is now Arizona, attacking other tribes as well as pioneers who trespassed on Apache lands. That year, the American government established the Camp Verde reservation, but revoked and annulled it four years later. At that point the Yavapai-Apaches moved (unwillingly) to the San Carlos reservation. There they remained until the early 1900's when they returned to their homeland in the Verde Valley.

Near the reservation is Fort Verde State Park. Within the park is a museum that presents the "military side" of the 1870's Indian campaigns. Four remaining adobe buildings house artifacts from the soldiering days in Arizona. Along with military displays are Indian relics and tools of the early pioneers. The scenic Verde Valley is a fishing and hunting paradise. Nearby are three national monuments: Montezuma Castle, Montezuma Well, and Tuzigoot where prehistoric Indian dwellings and artifacts are preserved.

The Yavapai-Apache tribe operates a lovely visitors complex on I-17 where native crafts are available. Featured is a historical presentation of the Yavapai-Apache. The tribe also operates Cliff Castle Lodge and restaurant. Within the complex are superb paintings.

Fort Apache Tribe

SUNRISE DANCE

FORT APACHE

Whereas hot, arid, desert-like conditions are the norm on many of Arizona's Indian reservations, Fort Apache is an exception. It is nestled among some of the state's highest mountains, among them Mt. Baldy at 11,403 feet. On the extreme eastern edge of the reservation is Sunrise Ski Area which features six chair lifts on three mountains and a skier capacity of 7000. The reservation is surrounded on three sides by national forest, with the Mogollon Plateau on the north edge. Average rain and snowfall in a year at Fort Apache is more than 17 inches, as contrasted with 2.5 inches on the Cocopah reservation.

The people of Fort Apache are the White Mountain tribe. Traditionally the Apaches were mountain people, hunters and fighters of rugged build. They came to the southwest as nomads, raiding the Pueblo communities for food and supplies. In time they clashed with the Spanish explorers who ventured into the southwest and they also conducted raids into Mexico.

Approximately 8,500 people now live on the reservation, but nearly half the labor force is unemployed. Some of the major tribal enterprises are based on the reservation's large timber reserves; an 800,000-acre ponderosa pine forest is chief among them. Natives run the tribe's large sawmill as well as the ski resort which is the second largest employer on the reservation.

Jeanne Broome NAVAJO CRAFTS W/APACHE BURDEN BASKET

A particularly intriguing Apache craft is the "Burden Basket." These substantially constructed baskets are about 18 inches deep and the same in diameter--deep enough to carry a variety of burdens. Hanging from the sides and around the bottom are several groups of rawhide strands. The tribe is also known for its beadwork.

TONTO APACHE

Beadwork of much acclaim is produced by natives from the tiny Tonto Apache reservation. Every year on the Fourth of July, Apache craftsmen have a chance to display their products at a softball tournament attended by teams from all over the state. This is one of eight such tournaments during the year.

At other times, crafts are on sale at the Tonto Apache Market or at the community building. Like most Arizona tribes, contemporary arts and crafts are produced primarily for sale rather than family use.

This is a new reservation, established in 1972 on 85 acres near the town of Payson. The population is about 100 and natives find work in tribal-related jobs or at the lumber mill in Payson. The climate here is cool (average temperature about 72°), with elevation just over 5000 feet.

The tribal economy benefits from its location in beautiful Tonto National Forest. There is much tourist traffic bound for the Mogollon Rim area. Payson, a town of over 5,000, is a popular stop for travelers.

SAN CARLOS

According to Apache tradition, all forces of the earth and sky have souls. At one time Thunder Beings lived with the people. These supernatural hunters used lightning bolts with tips made of flint. Usen, who made the universe, is thought to have the greatest influence over the people. These are just a few of the wonderful hierarchy of mythological figures in Apache culture.

Apache ceremonials and beliefs are much like those of the Navajo. Rituals for curing the sick and blessing souls are most common. A shaman, who acts as both priest and doctor, has traditionally been the spiritual leader of the tribe. The most elaborate ceremonial is the Mountain Spirit Dance, held each summer, which celebrates the rite of puberty in girls. This is an expensive event for the family. A tipi is built especially for the girl and taken down after four days of festivities. During this time she is believed to have special powers which enable her to heal the sick by touching them. The girl's family stays with her for nine days, at which time she is given a yucca bath to purify her and she becomes eligible for marriage.

Today San Carlos is home to more than 7,000 Apache Indians. But when the 2,854-square mile reservation was first established in 1871, it was a relocation site for Mohave and Yuma tribes as well. The Apaches first came to this region in the 900's A.D.

Jimmie Woods   SAN CARLOS PRINCESS

In the Zuni language, "Apache" means "enemy," and the tribe developed a reputation for being fierce warriors. Although they never used horses extensively, the San Carlos Apaches were involved in some of the most savage fighting against white settlers in the early west.

San Carlos Apaches have a tradition of making fine baskets. Very early they developed a method for waterproofing their baskets with a pitch sealer. Basketry is still an important craft, but jewelry is equally important. The specialty at San Carlos is peridot jewelry. This transparent-greenish gemstone, a beautiful variety of olivine, is mined on the reservation.

Unemployment at San Carlos is high, running about 60% in recent years. Those who are working are generally employed in tribal enterprises such as the manufacture of jojoba bean oil or in government administration. Cattle raising and livestock sales also contribute to the tribal economy.

The San Carlos reservation is blessed with dozens of ponds and lakes, a real fisherman's haven. The canyon of the Salt River is considered by some to be as spectacular as the Grand Canyon, on a smaller scale.

FORT McDOWELL RESERVATION

Just 23 miles northeast of relatively wealthy Phoenix is an area of low per capita income and high unemployment. But the Fort McDowell community of 450-plus Mohave-Apache, and Yavapai Indians does have two major economic development programs initiated by the tribe. These are the Fort McDowell Ba'ja Bingo and Fort McDowell Yavapai Farm.

The reservation is a small part of the once-vast homeland of these native people. The Yavapais were hunters and gatherers who considered much of central Arizona their territory. All three groups--the Apache, the Mojave, and the Yavapai--were valiant fighters. Fort McDowell was a major post during the Indian Wars from 1865-1891. When the Apache Wars ended, the decimated tribes were moved to the fort, which was declared a reservation in 1903.

Fort McDowell can claim the famous human rights advocate Dr. Carlos Montezuma. Early in life, Montezuma was kidnapped by the Pimas and sold to an Italian photographer living in Chicago. His adoptive father sent him to medical school, but Montezuma's energies were focused on helping the Yavapai-Apache reclaim their native lands. He succeeded at this shortly before his death from tuberculosis.

Today's visitors to the reservation can attend the annual Pow-wow Trail of Tears Celebration in November. The Fort McDowell Indians are well-known for their basketwork.

GERONIMO & COCHISE

Two of the greatest Indian figures of the American West belonged to the Chiricahua band, the most feared of all the Apache tribe. What is today Chiricahua National Monument in southeastern Arizona was once the stronghold of these fierce fighters.

Although there had been occasional raids, trouble began in earnest in 1861 when Apaches abducted a white child from a ranch and chased off the cattle. Six Apache leaders were arrested, one of them killed. The chief, **Cochise**, escaped through the side of a tent but the other four were hanged. Vowing revenge, Cochise and his raiders waged 10 years of savage warfare against the settlers, escaping to Arizona's Dragoon Mountains when he was pursued by authorities.

To the end, Cochise fought to keep his people from being sent to a New Mexico reservation. He escaped in 1872, but was soon captured and surrendered. In defeat, he did move to the newly established Chiricahua reservation. There, two years later, he died. Today the county in far southeastern Arizona carries his name.

Geronimo, whose name in Spanish means "one who yawns," assumed leadership of the Chiricahua band in 1874 after the death of Cochise. Fiercely determined to keep his people independent, he resisted white and Spanish intrusion. When many other tribes were being herded onto reservations by the U.S. government, Geronimo refused to surrender. In 1876 he escaped from the San Carlos reservation and headed for Mexico. The following year he was arrested and sent back, but by 1881 he had escaped again. He and hundreds of Apache followers battled along the border against George Crook's army until, in January 1884, the Indians finally surrendered.

It was back to San Carlos for the Apaches, but not for long. In May 1885, 40 men along with 90 women and children led by Geronimo, fled the reservation and the desperate chase resumed. By the following March they had been captured in Mexico and again surrendered. This time a rumor spread that the Indians would be slaughtered once they returned to the U.S., so one last time they took flight--Geronimo and 30 of his people.

In Skeleton Canyon, Arizona, on September 3, 1886, Geronimo finally relented, becoming the last American Indian to surrender formally to U.S. authorities. He was exiled to Florida on the promise that he would one day return to Arizona. Instead, his band of Apaches were put to hard labor and never saw their homeland again. Geronimo died of pneumonia in 1909 at the age of 80.

Ramon Martinez   ALICE MANUEL, PIMA BASKET WEAVER

SALT RIVER PIMA-MARICOPA

The Salt River Pima-Maricopa Indian Community shares the heritage of two native American tribes, the Pima and Maricopa. The Pimas call themselves the "Akimel Au-authm" (River People), a tribe closely related to the Tohono O'odham. The Maricopa are known as the "Pee-Posh" (the People), whose origins are along the Colorado River, and they are linguistically related to the Yuman tribes there. The two tribes have been allies since the mid-1800s.

The Pima and Maricopa people farmed this region for centuries, using the highly developed irrigation systems of their ancestors, the Hohokam. Rich, green farm land comprises a fourth of the community's 52,000 acres. Other economic resources are sand and gravel mining, a cement plant, Cypress Golf Course and the Pavilions--the nation's largest commercial development on native American lands. The Pavilions offers shopping, theatres and restaurants.

The Pima are known for their meticulous basket weaving and the Maricopa for their red clay pottery. To venerate the accomplishments of the past, the tribes built the "Hoo-hoogam Ki" Museum, the name drawn from a Pima word meaning "house of those who have gone." The museum is dedicated to the Community's armed forces veterans. The main building is constructed of adobe, cactus ribs and desert plants--a rare example of the traditional "sandwich" style home built by the tribes. Ceilings are supported by mesquite tree columns. Exhibits feature baskets, pottery, pictorials, memorabilia and other historic artifacts from the tribes. At the museum's dining facility, visitors can sample authentic Indian foods while relaxing under the "Vahtho" (ramada). The Verde and Salt Rivers at nearby Red Mountain offer a striking natural contrast to the surrounding communities.

THE GILA RIVER RESERVATION

Just south of Phoenix is the Gila River reservation, homeland of nearly 12,000 Pima and Maricopa Indians. The Pima are thought to be the descendants of the Hohokam and followed their tradition of irrigated farming. But about every five years the area would experience a drought which made farming impossible, and the Pimas would be forced to hunt and gather berries and other foods to sustain themselves.

Because they were farmers, the Pimas generally had larger villages than their contemporaries. Casa Grande, a 13th-century four-story pueblo dwelling can be seen today, adjacent to the reservation. The ruins at Snaketown (on the reservation) are the best-known of the Hohokam architectural remains. Because the early Pimas had larger villages, they also had a stronger tribal organization than many other groups.

The Pimas were peaceful people. Since their traditional enemies were the Apaches, they were of great help to the U.S. Army as scouts during the Indian Wars of 1861-86. The Pimas also offered food and help to gold seekers traversing dangerous Apache lands during the rush to California.

The Maricopa are part of the Yuman group who were also a farming people. The Pimas influenced the Maricopa in many ways and the former even sided with them against other Yumans at times. They did not have such tightly structured communities as did the Pimas and they were a bit more war-like.

Agriculture is still a major enterprise on the Gila River reservation. Cotton, wheat, alfalfa and vegetables are among the largest crops. Amerind Agrotech Laboratories, located here, conducts research on plants which might have economic value. ATL is the world's largest developer of guayule (rubber) for commercial purposes. Another ATL product is devil's claw which is a type of fiber used in basket weaving. Pimas are well-known for their basketry.

The Maricopa are better known for pottery. But their craftsmanship is rarely as creative. "Form follows function" is the motto. Maricopa crafts were created to be functional, as were those of most Yumas.

Jeanne Broome · GILA RIVER HERITAGE PARK DISPLAY

Today, industrial parks are an important part of the reservation's income. Three such parks occupy the 372,000 acres. One of them, Lone Butte, is the most successful Indian industrial park in the U.S. Nearly 40% of the employment is in manufacturing-related jobs and another 11% in wholesale and retail trade operations. Still, unemployment is high compared to off-reservation labor figures; 32% of the Gila River work force is unemployed.

The Gila River reservation has two major visitor attractions, both easily accessible from I-10 at Casa Blanca Rd. The first is the Gila River Arts and Crafts Center which offers travelers an unequalled selection of Indian products. This is an excellent source for baskets, jewelry, pottery, painting and other native crafts. A museum is also located on the grounds. Nearby is the Gila Heritage Village and Museum. This center for tribal history offers tours of traditional homes from various tribes, the Pima and Maricopa as well as Apache and Tohono O'odham. Adjacent to this complex is the 50-space Casa Blanca RV Park.

There are many events in the Gila River community which are open to the public. Each year in March is the St. John's Indian Mission Festival. There is dancing, an art and craft display, and a selection of native foods. In April is *Mul-Chu-Tha*, the tribal fair, with a rodeo and parade in addition to food and crafts. This event is at Sacaton, a city of about 1,000 people.

Ak-Chin Indian Community   AK-CHIN FARMS ENTERPRISE

AK-CHIN INDIAN COMMUNITY

Tucked between the Gila River reservation on the
north and the Tohono O'odham on the south is the tiny
Ak-Chin reservation. From 500 to 600 people live on
21,840 acres here in the Sonoran Desert. Average
precipitation is just over six inches a year.

Two Indian groups live at Ak-Chin, the Pimas and
the Tohono O'odham (formerly Papago). The latter
were traditionally farmers who relied on flash floods to
irrigate their crops. Some have gone to raising cattle,
but many are still farmers. Eight percent of the
reservation is employed in agriculture. The biggest
employer is the Ak-Chin Farms Enterprise. The farms
are tribally owned on 16,500 acres and are highly
successful. In fact, all land on the reservation is tribally
owned, despite an earlier dictum for individual
ownership issued by the Bureau of Indian Affairs. Since
1988, the unemployment figure has dropped impressively,
from 38% to just under 4%. Likewise, the median
family income has increased to $11,125 per year.

The Ak-Chin reservation is just 43 miles northwest
of the Casa Grande ruins where visitors can see the
remains of Hohokam architecture. There is even
evidence of pre-Hohokam civilizations. People of the
Ak-Chin are known for their basketry; the Tohono
O'odham are the most prolific of all basket makers.

37

Jeanne Broome   JUANITA AHILL COOKING FRY BREAD

TOHONO O'ODHAM

For centuries the Pima and Papago Indians, named as such by non-Indian settlers, called themselves the "Akimel O'odham" (river people) or the "Tohono O'odham" (desert people). These closely related tribes lived as neighbors primarily in south central Arizona. But in recent years the Papago have reclaimed their traditional Indian name, both for their tribe and their reservation. Tohono O'odham was selected as descriptive of all of the 13 groups of O'odham known as Papago.

Over many generations the two tribes were peaceful agricultural people. Descendants of the Hohokam, the Pima developed practical systems of irrigation. They farmed more extensively than the Papago, perhaps because the latter lived farther south in more arid country, less suited to farming. The Papago's staple food was beans: tepary, mesquite, Palo Verde. Because of their developed farming systems, the Pima were more stationary and settled in permanent villages. Their tribal structure was more fully organized earlier than that of the Papago.

When the gold seekers came west in the last half of the 1800's, the Pima served them as scouts and helped them cross treacherous Apache territory. The Papago kept more to themselves. What interaction they did have with the white man was not to their benefit. Their sources of water, so precious to a desert culture, were

Jeanne Broome   SAGUARO HARVEST

allocated for other uses by the U.S. government. Soon
they were the poorest tribe in the southwest. Continued
contact with the white man contributed to a deterioration
of the Pima lifestyle. The reclusive Papago were able to
retain more of their traditional culture.

More than 16,000 people now live at Tohono
O'odham. Sells (population 3,000+) is the largest
community. The main reservation of 2,773,357 acres is
one of four sections of the Tohono O'odham. To the
north is the Gila Bend reservation; east is the San
Xavier; and west of the city of Florence is the third
section, tiny Florence Village. Various government
agencies are the reservation's largest employers. Cattle
raising and agriculture are second.

The Tohono O'odham still honor an old ritual in
the annual planting of crops. Toward the end of June
when the saguaro cactus fruit ripens, a wine is made
from the syrup. For three days it ferments in a "rain
house." The rain song is sung, there is dancing, and
headmen recite long poems. By then it is time to drink
the spirits and plant the seed.

SAN XAVIER DEL BAC MISSION

Basketry is the oldest of the Indian crafts still practiced today. The Tohono O'odham have, over the years, produced more baskets than all other Indian groups together. Necessary materials such as willow, bear grass, yucca, and cottonwood are now hard to find and even when available must be harvested at just the right time to produce high quality baskets. The earlier Papago were the only Indians to be successful at selling their baskets commercially and it is still an important source of income to reservation people. The Tohono O'odham also still practice the craft of pottery. One of the best places to buy these native products is at the Tohono O'odham All-Indian Rodeo and Fair held each year in October, or at San Xavier and Sells year-round.

There are many intriguing points of interest for the traveler at Tohono O'odham. Just south of Tucson on the section of the reservation that bears its name is the beautiful Mission San Xavier del Bac--"the White Dove of the Desert." The original mission, founded in 1692, was partly destroyed by fire, and portions were rebuilt in the 1700's. The building is still in use by the Tohono O'odham. Travelers may tour the mission or attend special holiday masses. Across the street is an extensive arts and crafts center.

Just across the eastern boundary of the reservation is Kitt Peak National Observatory, a center for optical astronomy, with more facilities for stellar and solar research than any other location in the world. Near Ventana is a famous cave containing bones of extinct animals which were thought to have been hunted by the cave's inhabitants more than 10,000 years ago. On the Gila Bend portion of the reservation, to the northwest, are the Fortaleza Ruins. This collection of 50 stone houses from the 13th century has been named a national historic site.

Pascua Yaqui Tribe   DEER DANCER

PASCUA YAQUI

Geographically you might think that the Pascua Yaqui reservation should be part of the Tohono O'odham. But culturally, they are worlds apart. Ancestors of the Yaquis were the Toltecs from Mexico who also settled many other areas of the southwest. It was in the late 1800's, after generations of fighting both the Mexicans and the Spanish, that the Yaquis finally moved north into Arizona.

For many years they had trouble maintaining their identity as a tribe. Finally in 1964, Congress allocated a tiny plot of land southwest of Tucson as a reservation. But it took 18 more years before the government granted tribal recognition. Today slightly more than 3000 Pascua Yaqui inhabit nearly 900 acres of reservation land. Another 2500 live off the reservation.

Yaqui children produce beautiful cultural paintings. Deer Dance statues are another hallmark of craftsmanship. Each year at Easter two religious societies of the Pascua Yaqui present an elaborate ceremonial. Members of one group are Christ's enemies with Judas as their saint. Each member holds the cross from his rosary in his mouth to keep the evil of Judas out of his heart. The other group are the "soldiers of the virgin." They wear costumes decorated with flowers and feathers. They "kill" the enemies by throwing flowers at them, the flowers being a divine protection against evil.

CALENDAR OF MAJOR ARIZONA INDIAN EVENTS

NOTE: This is a *selected* list of Native American events which occur on a regular basis. Months noted are approximate; exact dates may vary from year to year. For specific dates, contact the Native American Tourism Center (602) 945-0771.

January:

> **Ak-Chin Reservation:** Annual Election Barbecue

February:

> **Tohono O'odham Reservation:** Indian Rodeo Fair
> **Hopi Reservation:** Bean Dance

March:

> **Cocopah Reservation:** Annual Festivity Days

April:

> **Gila River Reservation:** Annual Mul-Chu-Tha
> **San Carlos Apache:** Sunrise Dances (ongoing thru October)
> **Fort McDowell Reservation:** Pow-Wow

May:

> **Hualapai Reservation:** Indian Day
> **Salt River Reservation:** Annual Senior Citizen Bazaar

June:

> **Hopi Reservation:** Kachina Dances (January thru August) sometimes open to the public

July:

> **Hopi** Annual Artists' Exhibition at the Museum of Northern Arizona in Flagstaff
> **July 4th Celebrations** at the following reservations: Fort Apache, Fort Mojave, Fort Yuma, Tonto Apache, Navajo
> **Annual Festival of Native American Arts:** Held at Coconino Center for the Arts in Flagstaff. Focuses on Arizona and New Mexico tribes.

Fort Apache Reservation: White Mountain Apache Tribal Fair

August:

Navajo Reservation: Annual Pioneer Day Celebration

Navajo Reservation: Annual Inter-Tribal Indian Ceremonial

Havasupai Reservation: Havasupai Peach Festival

September:

Navajo Reservation: Annual Fair, Rodeo, and Pow-Wow of the Navajo Nation

Pascua Yaqui Reservation: Recognition Day Celebration

Colorado River Reservation: National Indian Days

October:

Navajo Reservation: Western Navajo Fair; Northern Navajo Fair

Ak-Chin Reservation: St. Francis Feast, Catholic Church

Tohono O'odham Reservation: Miss Tohono O'odham Pageant

November:

Pasqua Yaqui Reservation: All Soul's Day

Fort McDowell Reservation: Orme Victory Celebration

Salt River Reservation: Red Mountain Eagle Pow-Wow

San Carlos Reservation: Veterans Memorial Fair and Rodeo

Gila River Reservation: Gila River Arts & Crafts Sale

December:

Colorado River Reservation: Annual All-Indian Rodeo

Pueblo Grande Museum, Phoenix: Annual Indian Market

Navajo Reservation: Christmas Arts & Crafts Sale

Tohono O'odham: Celebration of San Xavier

INDIAN ORGANIZATIONS
AND POINTS OF INTEREST

Amerind Foundation Museum
Dragoon, Arizona

An archeological research facility and museum devoted to the study of Native American culture and history. Includes the Amerind Art Gallery and Museum Store offering southwestern arts, crafts and books on history and Native American culture.

Arizona Commission on Indian Affairs
Phoenix, Arizona

An agency of the state government whose primary purpose is to work with other governmental agencies in assisting Indian tribes in developing mutual goals, designing projects and implementing plans.

Cochise Stronghold
near Benson in the Dragoon Mountains.

Among the caves and overlooks of this natural hideout, Cochise took his last refuge from the Cavalry.

Heard Museum
Phoenix, Arizona

Among America's finest museums, specializing in anthropology and primitive art, with special exhibits on prehistoric and contemporary Indians of the American southwest.

Four Corners Monument
near Teec Nos Pos

Four Corners, the only spot in the United States where four states meet. Indian vendors are usually at the monument selling food and crafts, including sand paintings and fry bread.

Gila River Cultural Center
Sacaton, Arizona

Museum, craft center and park. The park contains representations of Native American life in the Gila River Basin.

Deer Valley Rock Art Center
Phoenix, Arizona

Preserves over 1500 prehistoric Native American Petroglyphs. Guided and self tours.

Hopi Cultural Center
Second Mesa, Arizona

Exhibits feature Kachina Dolls, basketry and jewelry.

Monument Valley Tribal Park
Monument Valley, Utah

14-mile driving tour of spectacular red sandstone monoliths traversing through Utah and Arizona. Park is administered by the Navajo Tribe.

Navajoland Tourism Office
Window Rock, Arizona

Provides helpful literature for planning a trip to Navajoland.

Navajo Tribal Museum
Window Rock, Arizona

Exhibits center on the history and culture of the Navajo.

Pueblo Grande Museum and Cultural Park
Phoenix, Arizona

Remains of a Hohokam village and irrigation system from the 13th century plus museum exhibits.

Hubbell Trading Post
Ganado, Arizona

The oldest continually operated trading post on the Navajo Reservation, established in 1878. Now a National Historic Site offering handmade craft including pottery, jewelry and rugs.

Native American Tourism Center
Scottsdale, Arizona

Offers assistance in planning visits to reservations, makes referrals to Indian artisans and shops, provides Indian entertainers and demonstrations for special events, publishes a calendar of Indian events.

Native American Co-op
San Carlos, Arizona

Publishes the *Native American Directory*, the "yellow pages" of information on Native Americans, which includes guides for evaluating and acquiring Native crafts through trading posts and other outlets. Answers inquiries and conducts seminars on Native American concerns.

Many of Arizona's prehistoric Indian sites and museums are located in national parks and monuments. For descriptions, please consult ***Parks and Monuments of Arizona***, an Arizona Traveler Guidebook from Renaissance House.

Nearly all of Arizona's Indian reservations have museums preserving the heritage of their people, as well as trading posts offering native crafts and foods. Contact tribal headquarters (see listing next pages) for the locations of trading posts or museums on the reservations of your particular interest.

A note for summer visitors

The Navajo Reservation is the only area in Arizona which observes Daylight Saving Time.

Jeanne Broome   BASKETS: Hopi & O'odham

TRIBAL INDIAN COMMUNITY HEADQUARTERS

AK-CHIN
42507 W. Peters & Nall Road
Maricopa, Arizona 85239
Phone: (520) 568-2618

COCOPAH
Avenue G & Co. 15th
Somerton, Arizona 85350
Phone: (520) 627-2061

COLORADO RIVER
Route 1, Box 23-B
Parker, Arizona 85344
Phone: (520) 669-9211

FT. MCDOWELL
MOHAVE-APACHE
P.O. Box 17779
Fountain Hills, Arizona 85269
Phone: (602) 837-5121

FORT MOJAVE
500 Merriman Avenue
Needles, California 92363
Phone: (760) 572-0213

FORT YUMA-QUECHAN
P.O. Box 1899
Yuma, Arizona 85366
Phone: (760) 572-0213

GILA RIVER
P.O. Box 97
Sacaton, Arizona 85247
Phone: (520) 562-3311

HAVASUPAI
P.O. Box 10
Supai, Arizona 86435
Phone: (520) 448-2731

HOPI
P.O. Box 123
Kykotsmovi, Arizona 86039
Phone: (520) 734-2441

HUALAPAI
P.O. Box 179
Peach Springs, Arizona 86434
Phone: (520) 769-2216

KAIBAB-PAIUTE
HC 65, Box 2
Fredonia, Arizona 86022
Phone: (520) 643-7245

NAVAJO
P.O. Drawer 9000
Window Rock, Arizona 86515
Phone: (520) 871-6352

Jeanne Broome   SERI POTTER

TRIBAL INDIAN COMMUNITY
HEADQUARTERS

PASCUA YAQUI
7474 South Camino DeOeste
Tucson, Arizona 85746
Phone: (520) 883-5000

SALT RIVER
PIMA-MARICOPA
10005 East Osborn Road
Scottsdale, Arizona 85256
Phone: (602) 850-8000

SAN CARLOS APACHE
P.O. Box O
San Carlos, Arizona 85550
Phone: (520) 475-2361

SAN JUAN SOUTHERN
PAIUTE
P.O. BOX 1989
Tuba City, Arizona 86045
Phone: (520) 283-4587

TOHONO O'ODHAM
P.O. BOX 837
Sells, Arizona 85634
Phone: (520) 383-2221

TONTO APACHE
#30 Tonto Apache Reservation
Payson, Arizona 85541
Phone: (520) 474-5000

WHITE MOUNTAIN
APACHE
P.O. Box 700
Whiteriver, Arizona 85941
Phone: (520) 338-4346

YAVAPAI-APACHE
P.O. Box 1188
Camp Verde, Arizona 86322
Phone: (520) 567-3649

YAVAPAI-PRESCOTT
530 East Merritt Street
Prescott, Arizona 86301
Phone: (520) 445-8790